Dog Sweater Crochet

Step by Step Guide to Get Crochet Sweater for Your Dogs

Copyright © 2020

DEDICATION

Contents

Crochet Dog Sweater Tutorial for Every Size

Measuring Your Dog

First, you'll need to make all of your measurements.You can either measure your own dog or use the handy charts above from Pet It Dog Apparel to guesstimate the measurements. If you have a larger dog, then you can probably find some estimated measurements with a quick search :) Here is what you need to measure, along with a chart I drew up that might help:

(A) Collar (around the neck, loosely)

(B) Back (from the collar to where you'd like the sweater to end)

(C) Back Girth (around the back, leave out the tummy)

(D) Tummy girth (from side to side of the tummy, leg to leg)

(E) Tummy length (from bottom of sweater length to front legs)

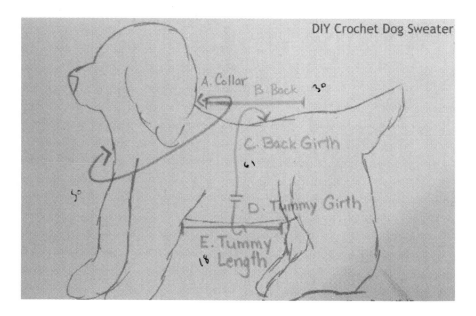

Now that you have your measurements, you can begin crocheting!

1. Cast on your yarn and make a chain the length of the Back (B) measurement. Be sure your back ends at a good point for both the tummy and back - as in, you don't want your dog weeing on the sweater, so don't make it too long ;)

2. Now you can use any stitch pattern you'd like to create the back of the sweater. I single crocheted in back loops only to make mine. I like making this sort of pattern because it makes the sweater stretchier. Crochet in each chain across.

3. Now continue to crochet in each stitch across until you have a rectangle piece measuring the length of your (C)Back Girth measurement (as in the photo above). This is the top of your sweater that will cover your dog's back.

4. Now you're going to create the tummy portion. Begin to crochet in the next row as you have been, but don't go to the end - only go until you reach you (E) Tummy Length measurement. Stop here and turn your work.

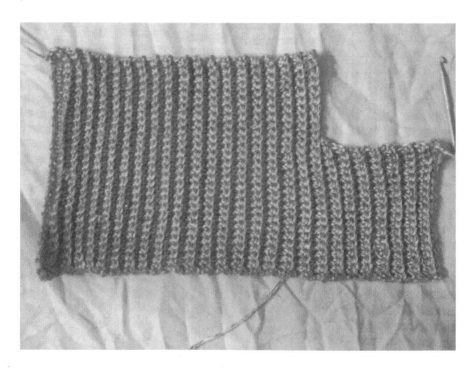

5. Chain 1, and continue your stitch pattern on these shorter rows until you make this small square your (D)Tummy Girth measurement. You can what I mean in the picture above. Now you

have to body of your sweater.

6. Now you'll sew the two ends together using your hook. Fold the tummy square over to the other side of the sweater so it looks like the picture above. Using your hook slip stitch the sides together. You can also choose to cast off first and sew the two sides together with a yarn hook, but I prefer this way since it's simpler and makes cleaner lines.

7. Now you'll be making your collar. Go to the front of your seater where the big opening is. Attach your yarn to the top of the rows (as shown) and crochet into the top of each row across. When you reach the end, chain enough stitch so that this whole side will measure the length of your (A) Collar measurement. Be sure to leave some extra lag here since you don't want it to be too tight if your dog ever gets stuck on something.

8. Once you have your length, attach your chain to the other side of the collar, where you attached your yarn. You now have a big circle the length of the collar measurement. Now you'll continue to crochet in rounds until the collar is as high as you'd like it to be. You can do one layer as I did, or you can make it longer and folded over.

And that's all there is to make this little sweater for your dog.

Easy Crochet Dog Sweater

Supplies:

• Lion Brand Vanna's Choice (Weight: 4/medium – 170 yds, 3.5 oz)

– Color A: Fisherman (#860-098) – 1 (1, 1, 2, 2, 2, 2, 3, 3) skeins

– Color B: Graphite (#860-407) – 1 (1, 1, 2, 2, 2, 2, 3, 4) skeins

• Lion Brand DIYarn (Weight: 4/medium – 65 yds, 1.05 oz)

– Color C: Red (#205-113) – 1 skein for all sizes

• Tapestry needle

• Size K (6.5 mm) crochet hook

• Stitch markers or safety pins

• (2-4) 1.5" wooden buttons (optional–see "Overall Notes" below)

Sizes:

XXXS, XXS, XS, S, M, L1, L2, 1X, 2X

Sample pictured is a size M on a 45 pound dog.

Choose your size based primarily on the dog's length from the base of the tail to the dog's collar and secondarily on the dog's chest circumference at its widest part. L1 and L2 difference is based on the length of of dog's back.

See sizing chart below to guide size selection. If between sizes, size up. For details on where to measure dog, see this website. A good rule of thumb is to allow space for two fingers between measuring tape and dog to ensure a comfortable fit.

Gauge:

Main Sweater: 13 dc x 7.5 rows= 4"

Ribbing: 13 hdc x 8 rows through the back loop only = 4"

Abbreviations and Glossary (US Terms):

ch – chain

dc – double crochet

dc2tog – double crochet two together

hdc – half double crochet

hdcblo – half double crochet through the back loop only

PM – place marker

RS – right side

sc – single crochet

sk – skip

st(s) – stitch(es)

WS – wrong side

yo – yarn over

Overall Pattern + Sizing Notes:

• Pattern is written and pictured with two options for fastening along side of dog's body. For dogs that don't mind having their legs put through a sweater hole, choose to seam the sides as described in finishing section. For more sensitive dogs, choose optional side fastener, which allows sweater to be buttoned around dog's legs. Reference Side Fastener section for details on how many buttons you'll need. (See photo of both options in blog post above as well as photo in Side Fastener section.)

• Pattern is written for smallest size with larger sizes following in parenthesis. Because pattern includes so many sizes, please go through and circle the stitch counts pertaining to your size before beginning. XXXS (XXS, XS, S, M, L1, L2, 1X, 2X)

BOTTOM RIBBING

Notes:

• Ribbing is worked sideways.

• Ch 2 at beginning of row does not count as a stitch.

• Row 2 and beyond are worked through the back loop only of the hdc stitches (hdcblo).

Using Color A:

Foundation Row: Ch 6 (8, 9, 11, 12, 13, 14, 16, 17).

Row 1: Sk 2 ch, hdc in each ch; turn. [4 (6, 7, 9, 10, 11, 12, 14, 15)]

Row 2: Ch 2, hdcblo in each hdc; turn. [4 (6, 7, 9, 10, 11, 12, 14, 15)]

Rows 3-16 (22, 25, 28, 31, 34, 34, 37, 44): Ch 2, hdcblo in each hdc; turn. [4 (6, 7, 9, 10, 11, 12, 14, 15)]

Do not fasten off. Rotate ribbing 90 degrees. Row 1 of Back piece will be worked into long edge of ribbing.

BACK

Notes:

• Row 1 is worked at a frequency of approx. 3 sc per 1 visual ribbing ridge (which is 2 hdc rows).

• Ch 3 at beginning of row counts as first dc.

Using Color A still attached:

Row 1 (RS): Ch 1, sc 26 (36, 40, 46, 51, 55, 55, 60, 72) along long edge, completing final yo of last sc with Color B; turn. [26 (36, 40, 46, 51, 55, 55, 60, 72)]

Using Color B:

Row 2 (WS): Ch 3, sk first st, dc in each sc; turn. [26 (36, 40, 46, 51, 55, 55, 60, 72)]

Rows 3-12 (17, 21, 25, 28, 32, 36, 41, 44): Ch 3, sk first st, dc in each dc; turn. [26 (36, 40, 46, 51, 55, 55, 60, 72)]

Note:

Decreases should begin when sweater length reaches from end of dog's back (where tail is) to approximately the front of dog's front legs. If you're finding the sweater piece too long, simply remove a couple of rows from the back section and move on to decreasing. Similarly, for a long, thin dog, feel free to add additional rows of double crochet before decreasing.

Decreasing:

Row 1 (WS): Ch 3, sk first st, dc2tog, dc in each dc until 2 remain, dc2tog; turn. [24 (34, 38, 44, 49, 53, 53, 58, 70)]

Rows 2-3 (4, 5, 6, 7, 8, 9, 10, 11): Ch 3, sk first st, dc2tog, dc in each dc until 2 remain, dc2tog; turn. 2 sts decreased each row

At end of Row 8, there should be 20 (28, 30, 34, 37, 39, 37, 40, 50) dc. Fasten off leaving 25" tail.

BELLY

Notes:

• Ch 3 at beginning of row counts as first dc.

Using Color B:

Foundation Row: Ch 20 (27, 30, 34, 37, 40, 40, 43, 52).

Row 1 (RS): Sk 3 ch, dc in each ch; turn. [18 (25, 28, 32, 35, 38, 38, 41, 50)]

Row 2 (WS): Ch 3, sk first st, dc in each dc; turn. [18 (25, 28, 32, 35, 38, 38, 41, 50)]

Rows 3-7 (10, 12, 14, 16, 18, 20, 23, 24): Ch 3, sk first st, dc in each dc; turn. [18 (25, 28, 32, 35, 38, 38, 41, 50)]

Note:

If you added or eliminated rows of double crochet before decreasing in the Back, considering doing the same thing with the Belly.

COLLAR RIBBING

Notes:

• Ribbing is worked sideways.

• Ch 2 at beginning of row does not count as a stitch.

• Row 2 and beyond are worked through the back loop only of the hdc stitches (hdcblo).

Foundation Row: Ch 16 (21, 23, 26, 28, 31, 31, 33, 39).

Row 1 (WS): Sk 2 ch, hdc in each ch; turn. [14 (19, 21, 24, 26, 29, 29, 31, 37)]

Row 2 (RS): \Ch 2, hdcblo in each hdc; turn. [14 (19, 21, 24, 26, 29, 29, 31, 37)]

Rows 3-18 (26, 29, 34, 37, 40, 41, 46, 53): Ch 2, hdcblo in each hdc; turn. [14 (19, 21, 24, 26, 29, 29, 31, 37)]

Fasten off.

SIDE FASTENERS

Notes:

• Side fasteners are optional. See "Overall Pattern + Sizing Notes" for more details.

• Ch 3 at beginning of row counts as first dc.

• For the 1X and 2X sizes, you may choose to add an additional button hole to each fastener to make it extra secure. To do this, work the Center Row (buttonhole) after you've completed Row 2 three times. Then work 3 more rows of regular double crochet before completing one more Center Row (buttonhole). Finish with 3 rows of double crochet and the last row as listed below.

Make 2 using Color B:

Foundation Row: Ch 8 (8, 11, 11, 11, 11, 11, 16, 16).

Row 1: Sk first ch, sc in each ch; turn. [7, (7, 10, 10, 10, 10, 10, 15, 15)]

Row 2: Ch 3, sk first st, dc in each sc; turn. [7, (7, 10, 10, 10, 10, 10, 15, 15)]

Repeat Row 2 another 0 (0, 1, 1, 2, 2, 3, 3, 4) times

Center Row (buttonhole): Ch 3, sk first st, dc in next 2 dc, ch 1, sk 1 dc, dc in each dc; turn. [6, (6, 9, 9, 9, 9, 9, 14, 14) and 1 ch-1]

Next Row: Ch 3, sk first st, dc in each dc and ch-1; turn. [7, (7, 10, 10, 10, 10, 10, 15, 15)]

Repeat Row 2 another 0 (0, 1, 1, 2, 2, 3, 3, 4) times

Last Row: Ch 1, sc in each dc. [7, (7, 10, 10, 10, 10, 10, 15, 15)]

Fasten off leaving 20" tail.

Fastener will have 5 (5, 7, 7, 9, 9, 11, 11, 13) rows.

FINISHING

1. Attaching Back to Belly: With RS of Back and belly piece facing, align last (top) row of Belly with Row 12 (17, 21, 25, 28, 32, 36, 41, 44) of Back (last row before decreasing). Pin if desired.

If omitting Side Fasteners: Working from bottom of Belly up on each side, seam approx. 1.5 (2, 2.5, 3, 3.33, 3.75, 4.25, 5, 5.25)". (See photo below.)

If including Side Fasteners: Seam Side Fastener to Back so that bottom row of Fastener aligns with bottom row of Belly. Take care to ensure button hole is on edge opposite of seam edge. (See photo in Side Fastener section above.)

This free, easy crochet dog sweater pattern fits very small, medium and large dogs and is perfect for winter! Easy pattern appropriate for beginners in sizes XXXS-2XL.

2. Attaching Collar: Turn sweater RS out. Align last row of Collar with top edge of Belly as pictured in photo C. Pin if desired. Using Color B, seam last row of Collar to top edge of Belly beginning at left edge of Collar.

Continuing with yarn attached, seam row edges of Collar to Back working across decrease section, continuing across straight edge, then across next decrease section. Finish by seaming first row of Collar to last row of Belly behind section that is already seamed and beginning with left edges of Belly and Collar aligned.

3. Collar Trim: Using Color C, attach yarn at bottom front corner of Collar. (See photo in blog post of sweater laying flat for more visual detail.)

With inside of Collar facing you:

Row 1: Ch 1, sc evenly around Collar edge, ending where Collar meets Belly inside sweater; turn.

Row 2: Ch 1, sc in each sc, ending where Row 1 began.

Fasten off and weave in remaining ends.

Bumble Bee Dog Sweater

Skill Level: Easy

Supplies:

1. Yarn: #4 Medium Worsted Weight

I used Red Heart, Super Saver Yarn for this project:

Color A - Black

Color B - Bright Yellow

2. Crochet Hook – I/9 US - 5.5 MM - 5 UK

3. Yarn Needle (blunt sewing needle with big eye)

4. Measuring Tape (for measuring your dog)

Stitch Abbreviations:

sc – single crochet

sl st – slip stitch

ch – chain

Finished Size:

13 inches long

8 inches wide

Pattern is made for a long, medium sized dog

Important Note:

Resources for Measuring and Crocheting Sweaters for your Dog:

Everyone's dog is shaped differently, and it can be frustrating when most dog crochet patterns (like this one) are only written for a certain sized dog. Because of this potential obstacle, several of my readers have asked me how to alter my pattern so that it would fit their dog. So instead of giving them an estimated answer, I researched and found a free eBook that will not only teach you how to crochet a custom fit sweater for your dog, but will also provide the instruction you need to modify any crochet pattern for your dog by using a simple measure-to-fit-pattern concept.

If you're interested, this free eBook is called "Custom-fit Crochet Dog Sweaters by Jenna Wingate". This is an affiliate link that will send you to Craftsy.com, but don't worry registration to Craftsy is also free.

Another great article which goes more in-depth on how to measure dogs for crochet sweaters can be found at DailyPuppy.com.

Here is an Idea for You...

If you really want to get creative, buy or make a pair of bumble bee wings to match and accessorize this crochet dog sweater pattern.

I made these wings for my dog and if you're interested in learning how to make a pair of your own, I could show you by video or written tutorial. Let me know what you think in the comment box below.

Crochet Dog Sweater Pattern Instructions

Beginning at Collar

Foundation Chain: With color A (Black) ch 6.

Row 1: Sc in 2nd ch from hook and in remaining 4 ch's (5 sc).

Rows 2-42: Ch 1, sc in each sc across.

Fasten off by leaving an 8-12 inch tail for weaving.

Whip stitch both sides of collar together by using a yarn needle.

Weave in loose yarn ends.

This Sweater Also Looks Great in Different Colors!

Pattern Instructions Continued

Upper Body

Note: Weave in loose yarn ends while you work.

Rnd 1: Attach color B (Yellow) to any sc space on long edge of collar, sc in each sc around (42 sc).

Rnd 2: (Sc in next 2 sc, 2 sc in next sc) repeat around (56 sc).

Rnds 3-4: Sc in each sc around.

Rnd 5: Attach color A, sc in each sc around (56 sc).

Rnds 6-8: Sc in each sc around.

Sl st into next sc and fasten off.

Middle Back

Note: You will now be working in rows.

Row 9: Attach color B into sl st, ch 1, sc in next 37 sc (37 sc).

Rows 10-12: Ch 1, turn work, sc in each sc across .

Row 13: Attach color A, ch 1, turn work, sc in each sc across (37 sc).

Rows 14-16: Ch 1, turn work, sc in each sc across.

Row 17: Attach color B, ch 1, turn work, sc in each sc across (37 sc).

Rows 18-20: Ch 1, turn work, sc in each sc across.

Fasten off, weave loose yarn strand into sweater with a yarn needle.

Leg Holes and Stomach

Note: You will now be working on top of the 8th round and on the 9th row.

Row 9: Skip 5 sc, attach color B into 6th sc and work a sc in same sp, sc in next 7 sc (8 sc).

Rows 10-12: Ch 1, turn work, sc in next 8 sc (8 sc).

Row 13: Attach color A, ch 1, turn work, sc in each sc across (8 sc).

Rows 14-16: Ch 1, turn work, sc in each sc across.

Row 17: Attach color B, ch 1, turn work, sc in each sc across (8 sc).

Rows 18-20: Ch 1, turn work, sc in each sc across.

Fasten off and weave in loose end.

Lower Torso

Note: You will now be working in rounds.

Rnd 21: Attach color A into the beginning stitch of the middle back, sc in each 37 sc around, ch 5, sc in next 8 sc, ch 5, sl st into the first sc that was made on rnd 21 (45 sc) (10 ch).

Rnd 22: Sc in each sc and in each ch sp around (55 sc).

Rnds 23-24: Sc in each sc around.

Rnd 25: Attach color B, sc in each sc around (55 sc).

Rnds 26-28: Sc in each sc around.

Rnd 29: Attach color A, sc in each sc around (55 sc).

Rnds 30-32: Sc in each sc around.

Rnd 33: Attach color B, sc in each sc around (55 sc).

Rnds 34-36: Sc in each sc around.

Hind End

Note: You will now be working in rows.

Row 37: Attach color A, sc in the next 37 sc (37 sc).

Rows 38-40: Ch 1, turn work, sc in each sc across.

Row 41: Attach color B, ch 1, turn work, sc in each sc across (37 sc).

Rows 42-44: Ch 1, turn work, sc in each sc across.

Row 45: Attach color A, ch 1, turn work, sc in each sc across (37 sc).

Rows 46-48: Ch 1, turn work, sc in each sc across.

Ruffle

Row 49: Ch 3, turn work (3 dc in next sc) repeat this pattern across row (111 dc).

Fasten off and weave in loose end.

Well Dressed Dog Coat

Supplies:

US-K, 6.5mm hook – Furls Crochet

75-250 yds Lion Brand New Basic 175 (75% acrylic/25% wool;

Worsted/yarn symbol "4"/UK:10-12 ply; 175 yds/160 m; 3.5 oz)

Color A: Plum – 1 ball all sizes

Color B: Whisper – 1 ball all sizes

Color C: Grey – 1 ball all sizes

Gauge: 10 sts x 7 rows = 4"/10cm in main st pattern

Sizes: Small (14" chest); Medium (18" chest) – shown; Large (22" chest); Extra Large (24.5" chest)

Helpful Links: Crochet Abbreviations; FDC – Foundation Double Crochet; Changing Colors for Striped Patterns; Carrying Yarn Along the Side

Matching Pattern: Well Dressed Cowl

NOTES:

In Piece #1 and the first half of Piece #2, stitch and row counts for the different sizes are written in the pattern as follows: Small(Medium, Large, Extra Large). Please mark the numbers that correspond to the size you are making before you begin.

Switch colors at the end of every row, cycling through colors A, B, and C – see linked tutorial above on Changing Colors if needed.

INSTRUCTIONS:

Piece #1 – Back

Row 1: FDC 24(26, 28, 30); turn. (24(26, 28, 30) sts)

Row 2: Ch 3 (counts as first dc here and throughout pattern), dc in first st, skip next st, 2 dc between previous and next st, *skip 2 sts, 2 dc between previous and next st; rep from * across, 2 dc in last st, turn. (26(28, 30, 32) sts)

Row 3 – 5(7, 9, 11): Repeat Row 2. (32(38, 44, 50) sts)

Here is a quick hand-drawn chart for Rows 1-3: Well Dressed Dog Coat - Piece 1, Rows 1-3, hand-drawn chart by Moogly

Row 6(8, 10, 12): Ch 3, skip next st, 2 dc between previous and next st, *skip 2 sts, 2 dc between previous and next st; rep from * across, dc in last st, turn. (32(38, 44, 50) sts)

Row 7(9, 11, 13): Ch 3, dc in first st, *skip 2 sts, 2 dc between previous and next st; rep from * across until 3 sts remain, skip 2 sts, 2 dc in last st, turn. (32(38, 44, 50) sts)

Row 8(10, 12, 14) – 19(26, 33, 43): Repeat previous 2 rows; break both yarns. Set aside Piece #1 until assembly.

Piece #2 – Belly

Row 1: FDC 6(8, 10, 10); turn. (6(8, 10, 10) sts)

Row 2: Ch 3, skip next st, 2 dc between previous and next st, *skip 2 sts, 2 dc between previous and next st; rep from * across, dc in last st, turn. (6(8, 10, 10) sts)

Row 3: Ch 3, 2 dc between first and second st, *skip 2 sts, 2 dc between previous and next st; rep from * across, dc in last st, turn. (8(10, 12, 12) sts)

Row 4: Ch 3, dc between first and second st, *skip 2 sts, 2 dc between previous and next st; rep from * across until 3 sts remain, skip 2 sts, dc between previous and next st, dc in last st, turn. (8(10, 12, 12) sts)

Row 5: Ch 3, dc in first st, skip next st, 2 dc between previous and next st, *skip 2 sts, 2 dc between previous and next st; rep from * across until 2 sts remain, skip next st, 2 dc in last st, turn. (10(12, 14, 14) sts)

Row 6: Repeat Row 2. (10(12, 14, 14) sts)

AFTER ROW 6, GO TO THE INSTRUCTIONS FOR YOUR SIZE BELOW:

Small Piece #2 Continued:

Row 7: Ch 3, dc in first st, *skip 2 sts, 2 dc between previous and next st; rep from * across until 3 sts remain, skip 2 sts, 2 dc in last st, turn. (10 sts)

Row 8 – 12: Repeat Rows 6-7; break yarn, go to Assembly instructions below.

Medium Piece #2 Continued:

Row 7: Repeat Row 3. (14 sts)

Row 8: Ch 3, dc in first st, *skip 2 sts, 2 dc between previous and next st; rep from * across until 3 sts remain, skip 2 sts, 2 dc in last st, turn. (14 sts)

Row 9: Ch 3, skip next st, 2 dc between previous and next st, *skip 2 sts, 2 dc between previous and next st; rep from * across, dc in last st, turn. (14 sts)

Row 10 – 15: Repeat Rows 8-9; break yarn, go to Assembly instructions below.

Large Piece #2 Continued:

Row 7 – 9: Repeat Rows 3-5. (18 sts)

Row 10: Ch 3, dc in first st, *skip 2 sts, 2 dc between previous and next st; rep from * across until 3 sts remain, skip 2 sts, 2 dc in last st, turn. (18 sts)

Row 11: Ch 3, skip next st, 2 dc between previous and next st, *skip 2 sts, 2 dc between previous and next st; rep from * across, dc in last st, turn. (18 sts)

Row 12 – 20: Repeat Rows 10-11; break yarn, go to Assembly instructions below.

Extra Large Piece #2 Continued:

Row 7 – 9: Repeat Rows 3-5. (18 sts)

Row 10 – 11: Repeat Rows 2-3. (20 sts)

Row 12: Ch 3, dc in first st, *skip 2 sts, 2 dc between previous and next st; rep from * across until 3 sts remain, skip 2 sts, 2 dc in last st, turn. (18 sts)

Row 13: Ch 3, skip next st, 2 dc between previous and next st, *skip 2 sts, 2 dc between previous and next st; rep from * across, dc in last st, turn. (18 sts)

Row 14 – 25: Repeat Rows 12-13; break yarn, go to Assembly

instructions below.

Assembly Instructions:

Step 1: Matching points A-D on the pieces as shown above, sew from A to B and C to D. Recommended method: whip stitch seaming

Step 2: Matching points 1-4 on the pieces as shown above, sew from 1 to 2 and 3 to 4. The seam should go from the back of the Belly piece toward the front of the coat for 1"(1", 2", 3").

Step 3: With Color A, sc evenly around leg openings, join and break yarn.

Step 4: With Color A, sc evenly around back opening, join and break yarn.

Now, isn't that snazzy!?

Size Small Dog Sweater

Supplies:

6.5 mm crochet hook

(#4) Medium weight yarn (Red Heart with Love)

Yarn needle for weaving in ends

Stitches

CH- Chain

SC- Single Crochet

HDC- Half Double Crochet

Half Double Crochet 2 together

Front Post Double Crochet – FPDC

Front Post Single Crochet – FPSC

-Note- I used a contrasting color for rows 4, 35, 38 and around the leg holes.

Get Started!

Row 1: CH 37, HDC into 2nd CH from hook, HDC across the rest of the

CH. (36 HDC)

Row 2-3: CH 1, Turn, HDC into each stitch across. (36 HDC)

Row 4: CH 1, Turn, 2 HDC into first stitch, 1 HDC into next 34

stitches, 2 HDC into last stitch. (38 HDC)

Row 5-6: CH 1, Turn, HDC into each stitch across. (38 HDC)

Row 7: CH 1, Turn, 2 HDC into first stitch, 1 HDC into next 36 stitches. 2 HDC

into last stitch. (40 HDC)

Row 8-13: CH 1, Turn, HDC into each stitch across. (40 HDC)

Slip stitch to Join the last and first stitch from the previous row. This will make it a circle instead of a flat piece.

Row 14-25 : CH 1, Turn. HDC into each stitch around, Join to top of the first HDC.

(40 HDC)

Row 26: CH 1,turn. HDC into the next 2 stitches. CH 8, Skip 8 stitches. HDC into the next 20 stitches.

CH 8, skip 8 stitches. HDC into the next 2 stitches. Join to first HDC. (24 HDC)

Row 27: CH 1, turn. HDC into the next 2 stitches. HDC into the next 8 Chains. HDC into the next 20 stitches.

HDC into the next 8 Chains. HDC into the last 2 stitches. Join to the first HDC. (40 HDC)

Row 28-31 : CH 1, Turn. HDC into each stitch around, Join to top of the first HDC.

(40 HDC)

Row 32: CH 1, Turn.**HDC Two Together. HDC into the next 8 stitches. Repeat from ** 3 more times.

Join to the first stitch.(36 HDC)

Row 33: CH 1, Turn. **HDC Two Together. HDC in next 7 stitches. Repeat from ** 3 more times. Join to first stitch. (32 HDC)

Row 34-37:(make sure you are working with the nice side of the stitches on the outside of the sweater) CH 1, **HDC into the next stitch. FPDC over the next stitch. Repeat from ** around.

Join to first HDC. (32 stitches)

Row 38: CH 1, FPSC into each stitch around. Join to first FPSC.(32 stitches)

HDC around the leg holes.

Attach yarn into one of the stitches of the leg hole. CH 1. – One HDC into each of the 8 stitches, each of the 8 Chains, and 2 HDC into the side of the HDC on both sides. (20 HDC) Repeat for other leg hole.

Weave in your ends.

Min Pin Sweater Paradise

Supplies:

Main Color (MC) 1 skein Lion Brand Vanna's Choice in Brick

Color A 1 skein Lion Brand Vanna's Choice in Dusty Green

Color B 1 skein Lion Brand Vanna's Choice in Rust

Color C 1 skein Lion Brand Vanna's Choice in Chocolate

Size E and Size F crochet needle or size needed to obtain gauge

Yarn needle size 2 3/4"

GAUGE: 15 dc and 10 rows = 4 inches with larger hook

STRIPES

1 row MC

1 row color B

1 row color A

1 row color C

1 row color B

1 row color A

Note: Change colors BEFORE the ch 3 at the end of each row.

Stitch counts are written for an average size min pin. Numbers in parentheses allow a little extra room if your min pin is a bit pudgy.

PATTERN

If you'd rather have this pattern in PDF form, click Autumn Sweater PDF.

Neck

Using MC and smaller hook, chain 8 loosely.

Row 1: Sc in 2nd ch from hook and each chain across. 7 sts. Ch 1, turn.

Row 2: Sc in back loop only of each sc across. Ch 1, turn.

Repeat prev row 44 (46) times. On last row, don't make the ch 1. Don't end off.

Shoulders

Switch to larger hook. Begin making stripes using pattern above.

Joining row: Ch 3 for first dc. Make 49 (53) dc along the long side of the neck piece. 50 (54) sts. Ch 3, turn.

Row 1: Dc in first stitch, inc made. Dc in each dc across to last stitch, 2 dc in last dc, inc made. 52 (56) sts. Ch 3, turn.

Rows 2 – 7: Repeat Row 1. 64 (68) sts. Don't end off.

First Leg Hole

Row 1: Skip first dc. Dc in next 7 (9) dc. 8 (10) sts. Ch 3, turn. Leave the rest of the row unworked.

Row 2: Skip first dc. Dc in each dc to end of row. Ch 3, turn.

Rows 3 – 5: Repeat Row 2. On last row, don't make ch 3. End off.

Upper Back

Go back to unworked stitches from first row of the leg hole. Skip the next 7 (7) stitches after the leg hole piece and join the yarn to the row.

Row 1: Ch 3 for first dc, dc in next 33 dc. 34 (34) sts. Ch 3, turn. Leave the rest of the row unworked.

Row 2: Skip first dc. Dc in each dc to end of row. Ch 3, turn.

Row 3 – 5: Repeat Row 2. On last row, don't make ch 3. End off.

Second Leg Hole

Go back to unworked stitches from first row of the leg hole. Skip the next 7 (7) stitches after the upper back part and join the yarn to the row.

Row 1: Ch 3. Dc in remaining 7 (9) dc. 8 (10) sts. Ch 3, turn.

Row 2: Skip first dc. Dc in each dc to end of row. Ch 3, turn.

Rows 3 – 5: Repeat Row 2. You will end at the edge of the work. Don't end off.

Remaining Chest

Row 1: Skip first dc. Dc in each dc along second leg hole. Loosely ch 7. Dc in each dc across upper back section. Loosely ch 7. Dc in each dc on first leg hole. Ch 3, turn.

Row 2: Skip first dc. Dc in each dc and ch across. 62 (66) sts. Ch 3, turn.

Row 3: Skip first dc. Dc in each dc across. Ch 3, turn.

Repeat Row 3 until piece measures 3 ½ inches from the bottom of the leg hole to the last row worked. Don't end off.

Waist and Lower Back

Row 1: Slip st in next 15 (15) dc. Ch 3. Dc in next 31 (35) dc. 32 (36) sts. Ch 3, turn. You should have 15 dc remaining unworked for the row.

Row 2: Skip first dc. Dc2tog, dc in each dc across to second to last dc, dc2tog. 30 (34) sts. Ch 3, turn.

Row 3: Repeat Row 2. 28 (32) sts.

Row 4: Skip first dc. Dc in each dc across. Ch 3, turn.

Row 5 – 6: Repeat Row 4. End off.

Back Ribbing

With MC and smaller hook, ch 10 loosely.

Row 1: Sc in 2nd ch from hook and each chain across. 9 sts. Ch 1, turn.

Row 2: Sc in back loop only of each sc across. Ch 1, turn.

Repeat prev row 25 (27) times or until length of ribbing matches the length of the lower back hem. On last row, don't make the ch 1. End off.

Stitch neck and chest seam, taking care to line up the stripes.

Raglan-style Leg Sleeves

With MC and smaller hook, working from the inside of the sweater, join yarn to corner of leg hole closest to neck band and chest seam.

Round 1: Make 13 sc in lower edge of hole, sc in each of 7 dc on left side of hole, 13 sc in upper edge of hole, sc in each of 7 dc on right side of hole. Join with ss to first sc. 40 sts. Ch 1.

Round 2: Skip first sc, sc in next 12 sc, hdc in next 7 sc, dc in next 13 sc, hdc in last 7 sc, join with ss to first sc. 40 sts. Join color A. Ch 1.

Round 3: Skip first sc, sc in next 12 sc, hdc2tog, hdc in next 5 hdc, dc2tog, dc in next 9 dc, dc2tog, hdc in next 5 hdc, hdc2tog, join with ss to first sc. 36 sts. Join color B. Ch 1.

Round 4: Skip first sc, sc in next 12 sc, hdc2tog, hdc in next 4 hdc, dc2tog, dc in next 7 dc, dc2tog, hdc in next 4 hdc, hdc2tog, join with ss to first sc. 32 sts. Join color C. Ch 1.

Round 5: Skip first sc, sc2tog, sc in next 9 st, sc2tog, hdc2tog, hdc in next 3 hdc, dc2tog, dc in next 5 dc, dc2tog, hdc in next 3 hdc, hdc2tog, join with ss to first sc. 26 sts. Join color B. Ch 1.

Round 6: Skip first sc, sc2tog, sc in next 7 st, sc2tog, hdc2tog, hdc in next hdc, dc2tog, dc in next 3 dc, dc2tog, hdc in next hdc, hdc2tog, join with ss to first sc. 20 sts. Join MC. Ch 1.

Round 7: Sc in each st around. Join with ss to first sc. Ch 1.

Round 8: Sc in each sc around. Join with ss to first sc. End off.

Belly Opening Edging

With MC and smaller hook, join yarn to edge of opening. Sc evenly around the opening and in each dc at the back hem. End off.

Finishing

Sew back ribbing to back hem. Weave in all ends.

Extra Small Dog Sweater

Supplies:

5.5 mm crochet hook

(#4)Medium weight yarn

Yarn needle for weaving in ends

Stitches

CH- Chain

SC- Single Crochet

HDC- Half Double Crochet

Half Double Crochet 2 together

Front Post Double Crochet – FPDC

Front Post Single Crochet – FPSC

Get Started!

Row 1: CH 37, HDC into 2nd CH from hook, HDC across the rest of the

CH. (36 HDC)

Row 2-3: CH 1, Turn, HDC into each stitch across. (36 HDC)

Row 4: CH 1, Turn, 2 HDC into first stitch, 1 HDC into next 34 stitches, 2 HDC into last stitch. (38 HDC)

Row 5-6: CH 1, Turn, HDC into each stitch across. (38 HDC)

Row 7: CH 1, Turn, 2 HDC into first stitch, 1 HDC into next 17 stitches, 2 HDC into next stitch. 1 HDC into next 19 stitches.

Row 8-11: CH 1, Turn, HDC into each stitch across. (40 HDC)

Slip stitch to Join the last and first stitch from the previous row. This will make it a circle instead of a flat piece.

Row 12-23 : CH 1, Turn. HDC into each stitch around, Join to top of the first HDC.

(40 HDC)

Row 24: CH 1, HDC into the next 3 stitches. CH 7, Skip 7 stitches. HDC into the next 20 stitches.

CH 7, skip 7 stitches. HDC into the next 3 stitches. Join to first HDC. (26 HDC)

Row 25: CH 1, HDC into the next 3 stitches. HDC into the next 7 Chains. HDC into the next 20 stitches.

HDC into the next 7 Chains. HDC into the last 3 stitches. Join to the first HDC. (40 HDC)

Row 26-28 : CH 1, Turn. HDC into each stitch around, Join to top of the first HDC.

(40 HDC)

Row 29: CH 1, **HDC Two Together. HDC into the next 8 stitches. Repeat from ** 3 more times.

Join to the first stitch.(36 HDC)

Row 30-33:(make sure you are working with the nice side of the stitches on the outside of the sweater) CH 1, **HDC into the next stitch. FPDC over the next stitch. Repeat from ** around.

Join to first HDC. (36 stitches)

Row 34: CH 1, FPSC into each stitch around. Join to first FPSC.(36 stitches)

HDC around the leg holes.

Attach yarn into one of the stitches of the leg hole. CH 1. – One HDC into each of the 7 stitches, each of the 7 Chains, and 2 HDC into the side of the HDC on both sides. (18 HDC) Repeat for the other leg hole.

Weave in your ends.

Spring Striped Dog Sweater With Collar

Striped Dog Sweater with Collar

Ch 33

Row 1: with MC dc in 4th chain from hook. Dc in each chain across. turn

Row 2-4: ch 3 (count as first dc). Dc in same space as ch 3. Dc in each dc across. 2 dc in last dc. Turn b

Row 5-6: change color to CC. repeat row 2

Row 7-10: change to MC. Repeat row 2

Row 11-12: change to CC. Repeat row 2

Row 13- 16: change to MC. Repeat row 2

Row 17-18: change to CC. Repeat row 2. Join with sl st.

Round 19-22: change to MC. ch 3. Dc across. Join with sl st

Round 23: change to CC. Ch 3. Dc across. Join with sl st

Round 24: ch 1. sc in next 3. Ch 12. Sc next 32. Ch 12. Sc next 4. Join with sl st

Round 25: ch 1. Sc in next 3 sc. Sc in next 12 ch. Sc in next 4 sc. Join with sl st

Round 26: change to MC. Ch 3. Dc across. Join with sl st

Round 27-29: ch 3. Decrese by 1. Dc across. Dcrese by 1. Join with sl st

Round 30-31: change to CC. Repeat row 29

Round 32-33: ch 3. Dc around. Join with sl st

Row 34-37: ch 3. Dc in same space as ch 3. Dc around. 2 dc in last dc. Do not join. Turn

Tie off. Weave ends in.

Printed in Great Britain
by Amazon